INSIDE THE OCD MIND

POV CINDY ALVES

SREETAMA HALDER

BlueRose ONE
Stories Matter
NewDelhi • London

BLUEROSE PUBLISHERS
India | U.K.

Copyright © Sreetama Halder 2023

All rights reserved by author. No part of this publication may be reproduced, stored in a retrieval system or transmitted in any form or by any means, electronic, mechanical, photocopying, recording or otherwise, without the prior permission of the author. Although every precaution has been taken to verify the accuracy of the information contained herein, the publisher assumes no responsibility for any errors or omissions. No liability is assumed for damages that may result from the use of information contained within.

BlueRose Publishers takes no responsibility for any damages, losses, or liabilities that may arise from the use or misuse of the information, products, or services provided in this publication.

For permissions requests or inquiries regarding this publication, please contact:

BLUEROSE PUBLISHERS
www.BlueRoseONE.com
info@bluerosepublishers.com
+91 8882 898 898
+4407342408967

ISBN: 978-93-5819-343-5

Cover design: Muskan Sachdeva
Typesetting: Rohit

First Edition: October 2023

Contents

Introduction 1
Dermatillomania 4
The scars..6
Compulsive eating..8
Am I fat?..10
Kleptomania..12
Delinquency 13
Cleanliness 16
Clean freak 18
Trichotillomania..21
Miss Baldy...23
Limerence 26
Taboo love...28

Introduction

In the shadows of desires and secret joys, Cindy finds herself entangled in a world of emotions that might seem unfathomable to most. She's no celebrity or extraordinary figure, just a protagonist in this tale, urging you to delve into the depths of her psyche and bear witness to her journey.

Greetings, dear readers, I am Cindy Alves, a mere 18-year-old maiden. On the surface, I may appear like any other ordinary being, but there's a mysterious aspect to my life that I am not yet ready to unveil. A hidden secret that holds the key to understanding my very essence, a secret that will only unravel as you traverse the winding paths of my life story. "Tee-hee," I chuckle, for the intrigue of my tale lies in the enigmatic revelations that lie ahead.

As you walk alongside me in this narrative, you'll discover the relentless tugs of emotions that have guided my choices, leading me down uncharted territories of joy and longing. I yearn to share my voice with you, to expose the intricacies of human emotions that often elude the light of day.

My story is not one of grandeur or fame, but rather a mosaic of everyday emotions, dreams, and desires that resonate with the heart of every individual. In my vulnerability, I hope to shed light on the common threads that bind us all together as human beings.

So, embark on this journey with me, dear readers, and together, let us explore the tapestry of my soul, where passions and yearnings intertwine, and where the untold wonders of the human experience await. I invite you to witness the unveiling of my secret and to discover the true essence of Cindy Alves.

In the simple questions lies a profound revelation, a glimpse into the inner workings of our shared humanity. But before we embark on this journey together, promise me that you'll see the world through my eyes.

My eyes are no different from yours, gifted with the same organs by a divine hand. I am no beholder of superhuman visions, just an ordinary soul trying to make sense of a complex world. Yet, within the depths of my being, a relentless struggle unravels, one that is both familiar and deeply personal.

You see, sometimes a shadowy presence takes hold of my mind, a force beyond my control. It is not a ghostly apparition that haunts me, nor a mere feeling of anxiety that grips my heart. It is something more, something that intertwines with the fabric of my being— OCD, the uninvited guest that lurks within.

I WOULD LIKE TO ASK YOU CERTAIN QUESTIONS:

1. Do you like to eat scrumptious food all alone?

2. Do you like to keep yourself and your environment clean and tidy?

3. What do you do when your needs are not met?

4. Have you ever fallen in love for someone?
5. Do you like the taste of blood?
6. Does your skin itch?

Now, you might wonder why such fruitless questions were asked. But in their simplicity, they mirror the complexities that come to define my life.

So, as you peer into the window of my soul, remember that within each seemingly fruitless question lies a tale of triumph and tribulation, a dance of light and shadow. I invite you to see the world through my eyes, to embrace the intricacies of my journey, and to discover the beauty in vulnerability. For it is in understanding one another that we find our shared humanity, woven together in the tapestry of life.

Dermatillomania

Skin picking, medically known as dermatillomania or excoriation disorder, is a compulsive behaviour characterized by the repetitive picking, scratching, or digging into one's own skin. It is an impulse control disorder and often falls under the category of body-focused repetitive behaviours (BFRBs).

Individuals who suffer from skin picking may find it challenging to resist the urge to pick at their skin, leading to the creation of wounds, sores, or lesions. The areas most commonly targeted are those that can be easily reached and concealed, such as the face, arms, hands, and legs.

The act of skin picking often starts as a response to feelings of stress, anxiety, boredom, or even excitement. Engaging in this behaviour may provide a temporary sense of relief or comfort, but it can quickly become a self-perpetuating cycle. Feelings of guilt, shame, or embarrassment may follow the picking episode, causing further distress and perpetuating the urge to pick as a way to cope with negative emotions.

The consequences of skin picking can be physically and emotionally damaging. Repeated picking can lead to infections, scarring, and delayed healing of wounds. The skin may become inflamed, red, and painful, exacerbating the urge to pick as a way to alleviate discomfort, thus reinforcing the behaviour.

For those who suffer from skin picking, the behaviour can become a significant source of distress and impairment in daily life. It may lead to social isolation, reduced self-esteem, and a reluctance to engage in activities that draw attention to the affected areas.

Addressing skin picking often involves a multifaceted approach, including therapy (such as cognitive-behavioral therapy), support groups, and, in some cases, medication.

The scars

In the dimly lit room, I sat on the edge of my bed, fingers restlessly tracing invisible patterns on my lap. Moonlight filtered through the half-closed curtains, casting ethereal shadows across my face. A feeling of unease settled upon me, the kind that gnawed at me like an insatiable hunger.

With a deep breath, I moved my hand to my head, my nails lightly grazing my scalp. The sensation sent a shiver down my spine, simultaneously soothing and invigorating. My fingertips found a spot, a tender place where thoughts seemed to congregate like a gathering storm.

As if pulled by an invisible force, my nails dug into the scalp, a rush of mixed emotions overwhelming my senses. Pain mingled with relief, like a bittersweet melody playing within my soul. I winced as blood rose to the surface, but there was a strange allure in seeing my emotions manifest in such a tangible way.

Each scrape, each pull of skin, seemed to peel away the layers I hid beneath. My hair fell in disarray around me, like a dark curtain shielding me from the world. The more I picked, the more my mind spiralled into an almost trance-like state, the outside world fading away as if it were merely a distant echo.

In the silence of the room, I could hear the faint rustling of my breath, the sound of my heartbeat pounding in my ears. It was as if my whole body was protesting against the assault it endured, yet my mind seemed deaf to its pleas.

As the minutes stretched into what felt like hours, my fingers became coated with my own life force. My head throbbed, the pain intermingling with an odd sense of gratification. The raw, red patches on my scalp bore witness to the emotional tempest that raged within.

Finally, exhaustion washed over me like a tidal wave, and I let my hands fall to my sides, my body trembling with a mix of adrenaline and despair. The aftermath of my actions lay scattered around me, a haunting reminder of the darkness I grappled with.

In the stillness of the night, I felt a sense of both emptiness and catharsis. The picking had offered temporary respite, a momentary escape from the tangled web of my emotions. But as the moon's glow faded, so did the fleeting solace, leaving me with a haunting question that lingered like an echo in the depths of my mind: How could I find true healing when the very act of picking seemed to anchor her to my pain?

Compulsive eating

Compulsive eating disorder, also known as binge eating disorder (BED), is a serious mental health condition characterized by recurrent episodes of uncontrollable overeating, often referred to as "bingeing." During these episodes, individuals consume large quantities of food in a short period, usually feeling a loss of control over their eating behaviour.

People with binge eating disorder often eat rapidly and to the point of discomfort, even when they are not physically hungry. They may eat alone, in secret, or feel ashamed and guilty about their eating habits. Unlike bulimia nervosa, individuals with BED do not engage in compensatory behaviours such as purging or excessive exercise to counteract the excessive food intake.

Binge eating episodes are typically accompanied by intense negative emotions, such as shame, guilt, or disgust, which further perpetuate the cycle of compulsive eating. These emotional distresses often stem from body image concerns, low self-esteem, stress, depression, or other psychological factors.

Compulsive eating disorder can have severe consequences on physical health, leading to weight gain, obesity, and related health issues such as diabetes, heart disease, and high blood pressure. Additionally, the disorder can significantly impact an individual's emotional well-being, social life, and overall quality of life.

Seeking professional help, such as therapy or counselling, is crucial for individuals with binge eating disorder to address the underlying emotional issues and develop healthier coping mechanisms. Treatment may involve cognitive-behavioural therapy (CBT), dialectical behaviour therapy (DBT), or other therapeutic approaches tailored to the individual's needs. In some cases, medication may be prescribed to help manage underlying psychological conditions.

Am I fat?

In the quiet sanctuary of my mind, there lay a sacred ritual that unfurled like a divine dance. For me, the act of eating transcending mere sustenance; it has become a symphony of sensations, a ritualistic communion with the universe.

With each morsel that touched my lips, my senses awaken to a heightened state of awareness. The taste of food is not a fleeting pleasure but an exquisite revelation of flavours that whisper ancient secrets. As the flavours swirl on my tongue, I can feel a sense of euphoria, as if my taste buds are channels to the heavens above.

In the dim candlelight of my solitude, the meal transformed into an intimate dialogue with my soul. Each bite seemed to nourish not just my body but also my spirit, as if I were feeding an insatiable hunger that resided deep within.

But beneath the divine facade lay a tempestuous storm. The act of eating becomes a frenzied symphony, an untamed rhythm that drive me to devour, to consume, to lose myself in the torrents of flavours. The boundaries blurred, and the ritual takes on a life of its own, an uncontrollable dance that ensnares me.

As the last crumb vanished from my plate, a sense of both satisfaction and longing washed over me like a tide. The divine ritual had brought me to a sacred place, but it is also a battleground where desires wages war.

In the depths of my being, I yearned for solace, a sanctuary free from the clutches of my compulsive eating. I knew that to truly find peace, I must confront the storm within and seek harmony beyond the bounds of her ritual.

In the depths of self-doubt, I find myself haunted by the question, "Am I fat?" The mirror reflects my insecurities, and every glance leaves me anxious about my self-image.

Thus, in the pages of my life's novel, I embark on a journey of self-discovery, where the divine ritual of eating becomes a mirror to my soul. As I unravel the threads of my obsessions, I learnt that true nourishment lies not just in the flavours on my plate but in the acceptance of my imperfections, the understanding of my emotions, and the embrace of my humanity.

In this sacred quest, I discovered that my relationship with food is not a reflection of weakness but a testament to my strength. And as I embraced my vulnerabilities with grace, I ascended to a higher plane, where the divine ritual of eating finds its rightful place—a celebration of life, love, and the intricate dance of the human experience.

Kleptomania

Kleptomania is a mental health disorder characterized by a recurrent impulse to steal items that are not needed for personal use or monetary gain. Individuals with kleptomania experience a strong, irresistible urge to steal, often feeling tension or anxiety leading up to the theft and a sense of relief or pleasure afterward. Unlike common theft or shoplifting, kleptomania is driven by an impulse and not by a desire for the stolen items. After the act, individuals with kleptomania may feel guilty, ashamed, or conflicted about their actions. Kleptomania is considered a type of impulse control disorder and may be associated with other mental health conditions such as anxiety or depression. Treatment for kleptomania typically involves therapy, counselling, and sometimes medication to address the underlying emotional and behavioral patterns.

Delinquency

Once upon a time, in the bustling city of Vienna, lived a young woman named Cindy. With her bright eyes and infectious laughter, she charmed everyone she met. But hidden beneath that radiant smile was a secret struggle that threatened to consume her.

I, Cindy have always been drawn to shiny things, the glimmer of jewels and trinkets, and the allure of beautiful objects. However, this fascination soon morphed into something beyond my control. An irresistible urge began to take hold of me whenever I entered stores or attended gatherings.

As if possessed, I find myself unable to resist the compulsion to take things that didn't belong to me. At first, it was small items—ornaments, pens, and coins—but the act of stealing offered me an intoxicating thrill that is hard to resist.

With each stolen item, however, a heavy cloud of guilt would settle over my heart. The initial excitement would give way to remorse, and the weight of my actions gnawed at my conscience like a persistent ache.

No matter how much I try to suppress the impulse, the lure of kleptomania proved too strong to resist. It is a cycle of desire, action, and guilt that seemed never-ending, leaving my poor soul trapped in her own torment.

As my guilt intensified, I began to withdraw from my friends and family. Slowly I became a master of deception, hiding stolen loot in secret corners of my room, afraid that anyone would discover my shameful secret.

One day, during a gathering with friends, the urge struck again. My heart pounded in my chest as I stole a precious necklace from a fellow guest. But this time, I was caught in the act.

My friend's eyes widened with shock and hurt, and my world seemed to shatter around me. The room fell silent, and I was confronted by my actions, exposed in my vulnerability.

In that moment, the full weight of my guilt crashed upon me like a tidal wave. Tears streamed down my cheeks as I apologized profusely, baring my soul to Jasmine, my friend and the other's present.

To my astonishment, my friend didn't turn her back on me. Instead, she showed compassion and understanding, realizing that my actions were driven by a deeper struggle. With her support, I found the strength to seek help.

Then, I embarked on a journey of healing, attending therapy sessions to address the root causes of my kleptomania. With time, understanding, and self-compassion, I learned to cope with my impulses and find healthier outlets for my emotions.

The road to recovery was arduous, but I emerged stronger, armed with the knowledge that I was not defined by my struggles. Now I use my experience to raise awareness about kleptomania, advocating for mental health and inspire others to seek help without shame.

In the end, Cindy's story became a testament to the power of empathy and the transformative strength of self-forgiveness. Though she carried the scars of her past, she also carried a newfound resilience, reminding herself and others that even in the darkest of times, the light of hope and redemption could guide them to a place of healing and acceptance.

Cleanliness

In OCD (obsessive-compulsive disorder), cleanliness is often associated with obsessive thoughts and compulsive behaviours related to excessive cleanliness and hygiene. This specific form of OCD is known as "Obsessive-Compulsive Cleanliness" or "Obsessive-Compulsive Washing."

Individuals with OCD may experience intrusive and distressing thoughts or fears about contamination, germs, or harmful substances. These thoughts are often irrational and disproportionate, but they create intense anxiety and discomfort. The fear of contamination may extend to everyday objects, surfaces, people, or even specific situations.

To cope with the anxiety and relieve the distress caused by these intrusive thoughts, individuals with OCD may engage in compulsive behaviours such as excessive handwashing, cleaning, or avoidance of perceived contaminated items or places.

For example, a person with OCD may feel compelled to wash their hands repeatedly and for extended periods to ensure they are "clean" and free from contamination. They might meticulously clean and disinfect their surroundings, or avoid touching certain objects or surfaces altogether.

Despite the temporary relief these compulsive behaviours bring, the anxiety returns, perpetuating a cycle of obsessions and compulsions. Over time, these behaviours can significantly impact a person's daily life, relationships, and overall well-being.

Treatment for OCD, including OCD related to cleanliness, often involves cognitive-behavioural therapy (CBT) and sometimes medication. CBT helps individuals challenge irrational thoughts, learn healthier coping mechanisms, and gradually reduce compulsive behaviours.

Clean freak

In the charming town of Vienna, there lived a young woman named Cindy. With her vibrant smile and a heart full of warmth, she was beloved by all who knew her. But there was a side to Cindy that set her apart from the rest - she was a clean freak.

From an early age, I had an inherent need for order and cleanliness. My room is a sanctuary of impeccable organization, with every item in its designated place. My friends marvelled at how effortlessly I maintained my space like a work of art.

In school, my neat handwriting and perfectly color-coded notes earned me the admiration of my classmates. The classroom seemed to brighten when I entered, bringing an air of tidiness wherever I went.

As I grew older, my cleanliness obsession only intensified. I couldn't bear the sight of even the tiniest speck of dust on my belongings or a misplaced item in my surroundings. My friends often teased me for my meticulousness, but I took it in stride, knowing that being tidy was an integral part of who I was.

My family fondly calls me "Miss Clean Freak," as I take charge of maintaining the house. Every surface shine under my watchful eye, and not a single crumb dared to linger on the kitchen counter.

However, my cleanliness pursuit wasn't all fun and games. As much as I enjoyed the order and tidiness, my obsession sometimes overwhelms me. I found myself spending hours scrubbing and disinfecting, unable to relax until everything is spotless.

One day, as my best friend, Sarah, visited me, she noticed the signs of exhaustion on my face. Concerned, Sarah gently asked me about my cleaning routine.

I hesitated at first, but the weight of my secret became too heavy to bear. I confided in Sarah about her compulsion for cleanliness and how it had taken a toll on my well-being.

To my surprise, Sarah didn't judge or ridicule me. Instead, she listened with empathy and understanding. Sarah reminded me that while my love for cleanliness is a part of who I was, it didn't define my worth. She encouraged me to find a balance, to allow myself moments of relaxation without the constant need to clean.

With Sarah's support, I embarked on a journey of self-acceptance and growth. I started to set boundaries for my cleaning routine, giving myself time to enjoy hobbies and spend quality moments with my loved ones.

As the days passed, I learned that being a clean freak wasn't something to be ashamed of, but rather a unique aspect of my personality. Embracing my love for cleanliness while also nurturing my mental and emotional well-being became my mantra.

Over time, I found harmony between my passion for tidiness and the joy of living a balanced life.

Now, Cindy is known not only for her neatness but also for her radiant spirit and the valuable lesson she teaches everyone about self-compassion and acceptance.

Trichotillomania

Trichotillomania is a mental health disorder characterized by the recurrent and irresistible urge to pull out one's own hair. This hair pulling can occur from any part of the body, but it is most commonly focused on the scalp, eyebrows, or eyelashes. Trichotillomania is considered a type of impulse control disorder and falls under the category of body-focused repetitive behaviours (BFRBs).

People with trichotillomania often experience a sense of tension or anxiety before pulling out their hair and feel a sense of relief or gratification afterward. The hair pulling may be done consciously or unconsciously and can lead to significant distress or impairment in daily functioning.

The exact cause of trichotillomania is not fully understood, but it is believed to be a complex interplay of genetic, biological, and environmental factors. Stress and emotional difficulties may also play a role in triggering or exacerbating the behaviour.

Treatment for trichotillomania typically involves a combination of therapies, such as cognitive-behavioural therapy (CBT), habit reversal training, and acceptance and commitment therapy (ACT). Medication may also be prescribed in some cases to manage underlying symptoms or comorbid conditions.

It is essential to seek professional help if you or someone you know is experiencing symptoms of trichotillomania. Early intervention and appropriate treatment can help individuals manage the condition and improve their quality of life.

Miss Baldy

With her gentle demeanour and radiant smile, Cindy brought a sense of warmth to everyone she encountered. But behind her cheerful facade, Cindy grappled with a hidden struggle that had haunted her for years - trichotillomania.

For as long as I could remember, I found solace in the act of pulling out my hair when stress and anxiety overwhelmed me. It began innocently enough, just a fleeting habit that offered momentary relief from life's challenges. But as time passed, the urge to pull became an unyielding force, a compulsion that I couldn't resist.

My once lush and beautiful hair started to thin and bear the marks of my constant pulling. The shame and guilt that accompanied this condition were burdensome, and I withdrew from social interactions, hiding behind hats and scarves, fearing judgment from others.

One day, as I gazed at my reflection in the mirror, tears welled up in my eyes. The realization that trichotillomania was consuming my life struck me like a lightning bolt. I longed to break free from its clutches, to reclaim my sense of self, but the grip of the disorder felt unrelenting.

My life took an unexpected turn after being named "Miss Baldy" due to my trichotillomania, a condition that compelled me to pull out my hair. At first, I felt devastated and embarrassed by the nickname, as it made me the centre of unwanted attention and ridicule. However, as days went by, my perspective started to shift.

In the face of adversity, I decided to embrace my unique identity rather than let it define me negatively. I began researching trichotillomania and connecting with support groups for people facing similar challenges. Through these connections, I found a community of individuals who understood me and my struggles and provided the much-needed empathy and encouragement.

With newfound confidence, I chose to become an advocate for mental health awareness and acceptance, especially focusing on conditions like trichotillomania. I partnered with local organizations and mental health initiatives to share my story, educate others about the condition, and combat the stigma surrounding it.

My story resonated with many people, and I received an overwhelming amount of support from my community. My courage and determination to raise awareness even attracted the attention of media outlets, granting me opportunities to share my journey on national television.

As "Miss Baldy," Cindy's presence at various events and public engagements became a symbol of strength and resilience. Her message of self-acceptance and empowerment inspired countless individuals, including those struggling with their own mental health challenges.

In her quest to make a difference, Cindy collaborated with hairpiece designers and stylists to create beautiful and fashionable headpieces for individuals experiencing hair loss due to trichotillomania or other medical conditions. These headpieces not only provided comfort and confidence to those wearing them but also became a fashion statement, spreading awareness in a unique way.

Cindy's advocacy efforts and growing social media presence caught the attention of influential figures in the beauty and fashion industry. She was invited to participate in runway shows and photo shoots, further breaking the mould of traditional beauty standards and promoting diversity in the industry.

Through her journey, Cindy discovered her passion for helping others and making a positive impact. She decided to pursue a career in psychology and counselling to support individuals facing similar challenges and encourage open conversations about mental health.

As years passed, Cindy's nickname "Miss Baldy" lost its negative connotation. It became a term of endearment among her supporters, signifying her strength, resilience, and determination. Cindy's story became a beacon of hope for many, showing that embracing one's uniqueness could lead to not just personal growth but also to creating a positive change in the world.

Limerence

Limerence is a term used to describe an intense and involuntary emotional state of infatuation or romantic attraction towards another person. It is often characterized by obsessive thoughts about the object of one's affection, a strong desire for reciprocation of feelings, and an idealized view of the person.

People experiencing limerence may find themselves preoccupied with the object of their affection, constantly seeking their attention and validation. They may also daydream about potential romantic scenarios with the person and feel a rush of euphoria or elation when in their presence.

Unlike genuine love, limerence tends to be short-lived and can be more focused on the idea of being in love rather than a deep emotional connection with the person. It can be an overwhelming and emotionally charged experience, often leading to feelings of joy or despair depending on the perceived reciprocation of affection.

Limerence is a common experience during the early stages of a romantic relationship or crush, but it can also occur in other situations, such as unrequited love or with someone who is unavailable or inappropriate as a partner.

It's important to note that limerence is different from genuine love, which involves a deeper emotional bond and a more stable and lasting connection. Limerence is considered a temporary and often intense state that may subside over time or evolve into a more mature and lasting emotional connection if the relationship progresses.

Taboo love

Once upon a time, in a quaint little town, two souls came into the world, destined to be connected in a way that transcended ordinary relationships. Meet Alex and Cindy, cousins who grew up side by side, sharing a bond that was both unique and deeply profound.

From a young age, they were inseparable, their laughter echoing through the fields and their dreams intertwining like vines. As they ventured through life together, their connection seemed to deepen, and they found comfort in each other's presence.

As they entered their teenage years, Alex and Cindy experienced a shift in their feelings. Emotions they couldn't quite comprehend stirred within them, and they began to see each other in a different light. Their once innocent bond took on a new dimension, and they found themselves yearning for more than just friendship.

At first, they dismissed these feelings as mere curiosity, the natural course of growing up together. But as time went on, the emotions grew stronger, and confusion clouded their minds. They couldn't decipher whether what they felt was simply limerence or something much more profound.

Their hearts were entwined in a dance of conflicting emotions. On one hand, they were drawn to each other, feeling an unspoken understanding that surpassed words. Yet, on the other hand, they grappled with the societal norms and the complexities of their relationship as cousins.

As their feelings intensified, they sought solace in each other's company, spending hours talking under the starlit sky, trying to make sense of their hearts' yearnings. They questioned whether their connection was simply an infatuation or if it was the elusive "twin flame" relationship that they had heard whispers about.

Alex and Cindy's souls were entangled in a web of emotions, and they struggled to navigate the maze of love and family ties. They sought advice from those they trusted, hoping for clarity, but the answers remained elusive, leaving them in a state of uncertainty.

One evening, as they sat by the riverbank, gazing into each other's eyes, they made a pact to cherish their bond, no matter where life led them. They vowed to remain true to their hearts, embracing the connection they shared, while also acknowledging the complexities of their relationship.

As they matured, they discovered that their bond was not a fleeting infatuation but a connection that ran deep in their souls. They understood that their twin flame relationship was not confined by societal norms or the boundaries of family, but a spiritual connection that defied explanation.

Their love for each other became a beacon of light, guiding them through life's challenges and uncertainties. They knew that their twin flame connection was a gift, a rare and beautiful bond that only a few are blessed to experience.

And so, in the heart of that quaint little town, Alex and Cindy's love story unfolded, transcending the boundaries of ordinary relationships. Their twin flame connection became a testament to the power of love, reminding them that true love knows no boundaries and that the heart always knows its way home.

In the quaint town where Alex and Cindy lived, societal norms weighed heavily on the idea of their love. Cousins being in a romantic relationship was deemed taboo, and the whispers of disapproval echoed through the streets like a haunting melody. Their families, bound by tradition, couldn't comprehend the depth of their connection and feared the repercussions of allowing such feelings to blossom.

As much as Alex and Cindy tried to deny their emotions, their hearts refused to obey the dictates of society. The more they fought against their feelings, the stronger their bond seemed to grow, like wildflowers determined to bloom amidst the obstacles in their path.

The weight of the secret they shared burdened them both. Each passing day, they yearned to be together, to openly embrace their love, but fear held them back. The love that was once their sanctuary now felt like a prison, caged by societal expectations.

Their souls were torn between what they felt was right and what their hearts desired. It was as if the universe conspired against them, playing a cruel game of fate. Yet, they couldn't deny the magnetism that drew them together, like two stars destined to cross each other's paths.

In the midst of their inner turmoil, they sought refuge in stolen moments. Beneath the moonlit sky, they would meet in secret, their hearts fluttering like the wings of butterflies. They cherished every stolen glance, every fleeting touch, knowing that their love was forbidden yet unable to resist the pull of their twin flame connection.

As time passed, the burden of their secret love grew heavier. The whispers of the town grew louder, casting judgment on their bond. Their families, blinded by tradition, insisted on keeping them apart, unable to see the depth of love that burned within their souls.

In their hearts, Alex and Cindy knew that their love was not a mistake, that the essence of their twin flame connection was pure and sacred. But the world around them refused to understand, shrouding their love in shadows of shame.

In the face of adversity, they had to make a painful choice. The love they had for each other was undeniable, but they also loved their families and their roots. With heavy hearts, they decided to sacrifice their own desires for the sake of peace and harmony within their families.

They parted ways, with tears streaming down their cheeks, their hearts shattered into a million pieces. The world seemed colder without each other's presence, but they held on to the belief that their twin flame connection would endure, even in the vast expanse of distance.

Years passed, and their love remained a cherished secret, hidden from the world. Alex and Cindy pursued their own paths, trying to fill the void left by their separation. Yet, the ember of their twin flame connection never dimmed; it continued to burn, a beacon of hope in the darkness.

And so, in the depths of their souls, Alex and Cindy held on to their love, knowing that in a world where societal norms dictated their fate, their twin flame connection would forever be a flame that illuminated their hearts, even from afar.

As the years passed, Alex and Cindy's lives took them on separate journeys. The town's whispers had finally ceased, and they both tried to move on, believing that the intensity of their feelings had faded over time. They convinced themselves that what they once thought was a twin flame connection was merely limerence, an infatuation that had blinded them in their youth.

Alex pursued his dreams of becoming an artist, pouring his heart and soul into his creations. Cindy, on the other hand, found solace in helping others and pursued a career as a social worker, bringing joy to the lives of those she touched.

Yet, even as they built their own lives, there was a void within them that remained unfulfilled. They missed the sense of belonging they once found in each other's presence, but they attributed these feelings to nostalgia rather than true love.

One day, fate brought them together again, unexpectedly. As they sat across from each other in a coffee shop, old memories flooded back. They reminisced about their stolen moments beneath the moonlight, their secret glances, and their unspoken connection.

As they spoke, they realized that the bond they shared ran deeper than they had ever acknowledged. The joy of reuniting brought a flutter of excitement, and they couldn't help but wonder if the embers of their love were still alive.

As the days turned into weeks, Alex and Cindy spent more time together, rekindling their friendship. They shared laughter and heartache, and they began to confide in each other as they once did in their youth. But amidst the joy of their reunion, there lingered a sense of uncertainty.

They questioned whether their feelings were genuine or merely remnants of their past infatuation. The lines between twin flame connection and limerence blurred, leaving them both in a state of confusion.

One evening, as they stood by the riverbank, the moon's reflection shimmering on the water's surface, they decided to confront their feelings head-on. They confessed their fears, their doubts, and their desire to find clarity.

In that moment of vulnerability, they realized that their love had evolved, transcending the boundaries of youthful infatuation. They understood that their connection, once mistaken for limerence, had matured into something much deeper.

They acknowledged that their twin flame connection was a part of who they were, an integral thread woven into the tapestry of their lives. It wasn't a passing phase or a fleeting infatuation; it was a love that had stood the test of time.

With tears in their eyes and hearts laid bare, they embraced their truth. They decided to let go of the need to label their feelings, recognizing that love could be complex, defying easy definitions.

As they stood hand in hand beneath the moonlit sky, they knew that their love story was not one of fairy tales, but of resilience and growth. They were no longer afraid of the past or uncertain of the future. Instead, they embraced the beauty of their connection, whatever form it may take.

In the revelation that their twin flame connection had never truly faded, Alex and Cindy found a sense of peace and contentment. Their love story was not conventional, but it was theirs, and they were ready to embark on a new chapter together, where love, in all its complexity, would guide them on an extraordinary journey of understanding and acceptance.

www.ingramcontent.com/pod-product-compliance
Lightning Source LLC
LaVergne TN
LVHW061605070526
838199LV00077B/7179